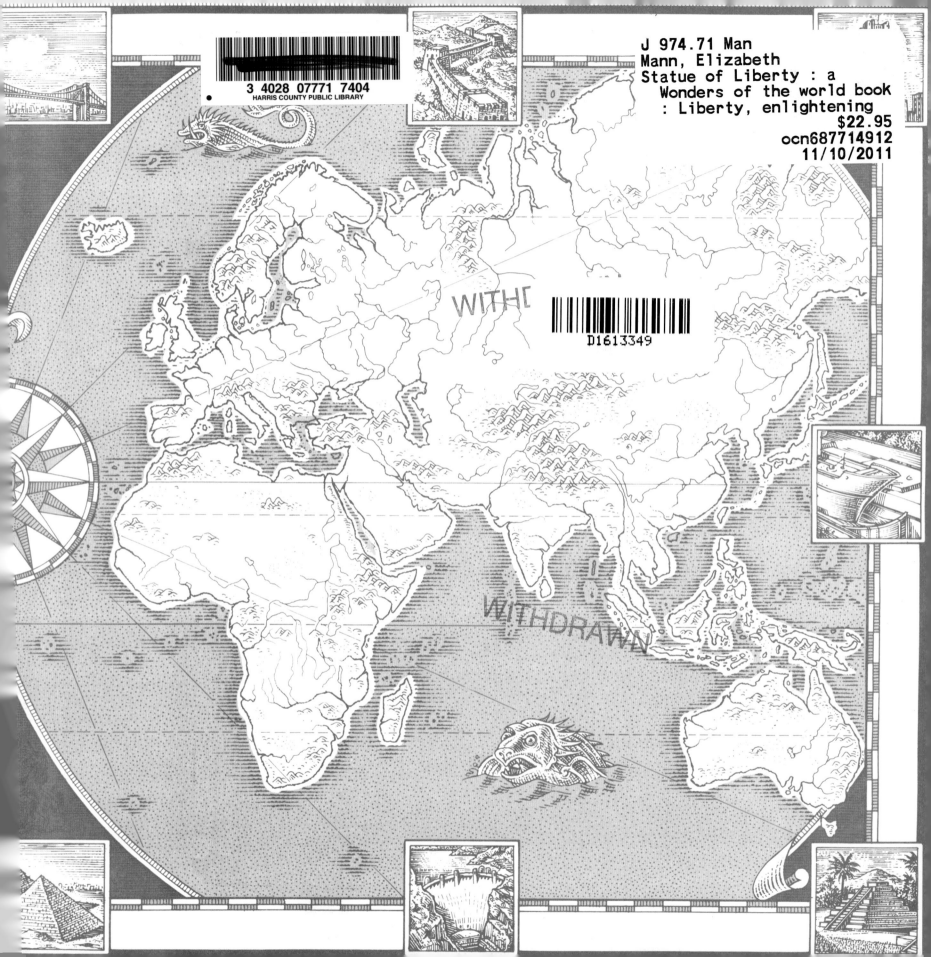

DEDICATION

To Lesley Ehlers, wise and talented designer, without whom this
book and many others would not have been possible.

ACKNOWLEDGEMENTS

Thanks to Barry Moreno, Historian, Statue of Liberty National Monument,
for research assistance and for careful vetting of the manuscript.
All errors of fact or interpretation are mine alone.
Thanks to Brenda and Joan for reading carefully and editing brilliantly.
And, always, thanks to Stu.

BOOKS BY ELIZABETH MANN

THE BROOKLYN BRIDGE
THE GREAT PYRAMID
THE GREAT WALL
THE ROMAN COLOSSEUM
THE PANAMA CANAL
MACHU PICCHU
HOOVER DAM
TIKAL
EMPIRE STATE BUILDING
THE PARTHENON
TAJ MAHAL

EDITOR: STUART WALDMAN
DESIGN: LESLEY EHLERS DESIGN
COPYRIGHT © 2011 MIKAYA PRESS
ILLUSTRATIONS COPYRIGHT © ALAN WITSCHONKE

Cataloging-in-Publication Data Available From the Library of Congress

Printed in China through globalinkprinting.com

Statue of Liberty

A WONDERS OF THE WORLD BOOK

BY ELIZABETH MANN

WITH ILLUSTRATIONS BY ALAN WITSCHONKE

MIKAYA PRESS

NEW YORK

On April 9, 1865, after four years of bloodshed and death, the Confederate General Robert E. Lee surrendered to the Union General Ulysses S. Grant. The Civil War was over—the North had won. The United States was still one country, and it was still a democracy. In France, many people rejoiced as if their own country had been saved. Edouard Laboulaye, president of the French Anti-Slavery Society, was one of them.

Five days later, when President Abraham Lincoln was assassinated, his death was mourned by French people everywhere. Everywhere except, perhaps, in the court of Emperor Napoleon III. The emperor had supported the slave-owning Confederacy during the Civil War and the Union victory angered him.

Laboulaye and 40,000 other French citizens wanted to show their sympathy to Lincoln's widow, so they made donations toward a gold medallion in the president's honor. When the emperor heard of the plans, he tried to confiscate the money. The medallion had to be made secretly in Switzerland and then smuggled to Mrs. Lincoln in America.

The inscription engraved on it read, "To an honest man who abolished slavery and saved the republic..."

To the people who contributed to the medallion, preserving the nation despite the horrors of the Civil War was as important an accomplishment as ending slavery.

ABRAHAM LINCOLN

"...an honest man who abolished slavery and saved the republic..."

The Constitution was the basis for the new American government and for the laws of the land. It has been in effect ever since it was written in 1787. President George Washington presided over the Constitutional Convention where it was created.

It was not surprising that French citizens would risk the emperor's wrath to show their respect for an American president. There had been a special bond between the people of the two nations for many years. During the American Revolution of 1776 a French general, the Marquis de Lafayette, volunteered to fight alongside General George Washington. Other French soldiers soon joined him. With France's help, America won independence from England. The success of America's war helped inspire the French Revolution of 1789.

Both revolutions had been fought in the name of liberty, but they had ended very differently. Once the Americans had broken free of the English king, they established a democratic government that was still strong nearly a century later. The French had overthrown their king, too, but then the country had lost its way.

Since the revolution many different governments had come to power and fallen in France—republics, monarchies, empires. There was even a frightening period called the Reign of Terror. Napoleon III patterned his government after that of his famous uncle, Emperor Napoleon Bonaparte.

No matter which government was in control, the bond between the people of France and the people of the United States remained strong. Through the troubled decades, many French people looked to America's thriving government in the hope that one day they too would live in a democracy.

The Reign of Terror began in 1793 just four years after the French Revolution. Thousands were put to death by beheading, and the guillotine became the symbol of the time.

NAPOLEON I

When Napoleon Bonaparte declared himself Emperor Napoleon I in 1804, he ended France's newly established democratic government, the First Republic, and began the First Empire.

In 1848 another revolution ended another monarchy and produced another democracy, the Second Republic.

NAPOLEON III

The Second Republic ended just four years later in 1852 when Louis Napoleon, Napoleon I's nephew, named himself Emperor Napoleon III.

EDOUARD LABOULAYE

Laboulaye was a prolific writer. He wrote a three-volume history of the United States and he translated the memoirs of his American hero, Benjamin Franklin, into French. He even wrote a satirical novel in which the main character swallows a magic pill and is transported overnight from Paris to America. Whether serious or satirical, the books were his way of sharing his love of America with the rest of France.

Edouard Laboulaye especially looked forward to that day. He had devoted his life to studying the United States and had become France's leading expert on America's history, government, constitution and laws. He believed that French citizens should have the same rights as Americans and he did what he could to make that happen.

He couldn't demand change in the French government—the emperor would have silenced him. Instead he worked indirectly by educating people about American democracy. Eager crowds gathered to hear his lectures. He chose his words carefully, speaking only about America's government and never criticizing Napoleon III's. To the emperor's spies, he sounded like a harmless scholar talking about a far-off nation, and they left him alone. Laboulaye trusted his other listeners to know that he was talking about the need for a new government in France.

Privately, Laboulaye spoke more openly. At a dinner with friends in 1865 he talked emotionally about the enduring friendship between the two nations. He proposed a gift to honor that friendship: a monument to liberty, to be presented to America in 1876 for the 100th anniversary of its independence.

Laboulaye's words would one day be remembered as the inspiration for the Statue of Liberty, but on that warm summer evening they were just words. Laboulaye's friends liked the bold idea, but they knew that while Napoleon III was in power it could never happen.

One guest at the dinner, Frédéric Auguste Bartholdi, was especially captivated by Laboulaye's idea. Bartholdi was an artist. In 1856 he had traveled to Egypt to study ancient works of art. The enormous stone sculptures, like the Great Sphinx, had a powerful effect on him. From then on, he specialized in larger-than-life statues, the bigger the better. He was already well known in France; a monument in America would mean worldwide fame. Even the ambitious Bartholdi had to agree that the time wasn't right. He didn't pursue Laboulaye's monument, but he never forgot his words.

In 1867, Bartholdi met with Khedive Ismail Pasha, ruler of Egypt. At that time, the 100-mile-long Suez Canal was being dug through Egypt to connect the Mediterranean Sea and the Red Sea. When it opened, ships would be able to travel between Europe and Asia without sailing all the way around Africa, an astonishing, world-shrinking event. The Khedive wanted to celebrate the opening by building a lighthouse at the entrance to the canal, a lighthouse that would be a giant statue. He had already chosen a name for it—*Egypt Enlightening Asia*—and he wanted Bartholdi to design it.

For Bartholdi this was the opportunity of a lifetime. He had never attempted such a large sculpture. For two years he worked on *Egypt Enlightening Asia*, drawing sketches and making little clay models, but in 1869 he was forced to stop. The Khedive had run out of money—the statue would never be built. Bartholdi's disappointment must have been great, but he soon had even greater worries.

Bartholdi did this watercolor painting to show the Khedive his idea for *Egypt Enlightening Asia*.

In the aftermath of the Franco-Prussian war, there was violence in the streets of Paris and fires burned out of control.

In July of 1870, Napoleon III declared war on a neighboring nation, Prussia (now a part of Germany). Bartholdi's home province, Alsace, was threatened. He enlisted as an officer in the French army.

The war, known as the Franco-Prussian War, was a disaster for France. By September, the emperor and 100,000 of his soldiers had been captured. By January of 1871, Prussia had won. The reign of Napoleon III was over, but at a terrible cost. Prussia claimed Alsace, another province called Lorraine, and five billion French francs in war payments. France was in chaos, in debt, and once again without a stable government.

Bartholdi left the army, but he couldn't return to his former life. Prussian army officers occupied his home in Alsace. His studio was in Paris, but the city was too dangerous for him to return to work there. During this time of uncertainty, with no home and no work, he paid a visit to Laboulaye. Once again Laboulaye gathered his friends together, many of the same successful businessmen and prominent politicians who had dined with him in June of 1865.

At this dinner, it was Bartholdi who talked about the monument, and he spoke from his heart. Fighting in Napoleon III's misguided war had made him as passionate as Laboulaye about the need for freedom and democracy in France. He was still an ambitious artist, still eager for an international reputation, but the monument had taken on new meaning for him.

The candles burned low as the men around the table listened, transfixed by Bartholdi's enthusiasm. Yes, they all agreed, Laboulaye's monument should be built, and it should be enormous, in Bartholdi's style. And yes, they agreed, the time was right. France was struggling to establish a new government. By drawing attention to the ideas of liberty and democracy at this important moment, the monument could influence the kind of government France would have in the future. It was also agreed that to succeed in this grand venture, they would need American support. And so, with nothing to lose and everything to gain, Bartholdi set sail for New York.

On June 21, 1871, Bartholdi stood at the railing of the ship *Péreire* as it steamed through The Narrows between Staten Island and Brooklyn and into New York Harbor. The vast harbor opened out before him. Wide rivers fed into it. Buildings crowded its shores. Hundreds of boats, of every imaginable size and kind, churned through the harbor waters. The lively scene dazzled Bartholdi, but in the end, what caught his eye was tiny Bedloe's Island.

Others on board the *Péreire* probably saw a small, flat island with a stone fort perched at one end, but Bartholdi, looking through a sculptor's eyes, saw a pedestal. He knew instantly that he had found the site for his monument. It was the perfect size, and it was perfectly located—visible from New York, from New Jersey, and from the deck of every ship entering New York Harbor. In fact he could already picture the statue he wanted to place there.

Bartholdi spent six very busy months in America, and wherever he went he talked tirelessly about the monument. Even Ulysses S. Grant, now President of the United States, listened to his plans. Unfortunately, the Americans weren't about to give him money based on an idea. When he returned to France he had nothing more to show Laboulaye than his watercolor sketches of Bedloe's Island.

ATLANTIC OCEAN

BROOKLYN

THE NARROWS

STATEN ISLAND

NEW JERSEY

E'S ISLAND

Above: New York Harbor as Bartholdi would have seen it in 1871 was indeed a crowded, busy body of water.

Left: Bartholdi's watercolor painting illustrates his idea for the monument on Bedloe's Island.

It's possible that the news from America was not a terrible disappointment to Laboulaye at that time. A promising new government, the Third Republic, was emerging in France. Because of his knowledge of American democracy, he was called upon to help write its laws and constitution. This was the work he had waited a lifetime to do, and he devoted himself to it. The monument was dear to his heart, but establishing a democratic government in France had to come first.

Bartholdi, too, had other work to do. Paris was safe once again and he returned to his studio to resume the sculpting career that the war had interrupted. Yet busy as he was, he still found time for the statue.

Bartholdi was a practical man. He had worked for two years on the Khedive's lighthouse and he didn't want that effort to go to waste. He began with his design for *Egypt Enlightening Asia* and altered it to create *Liberty Enlightening the World*.

Bartholdi made many rough clay models called maquettes when he was experimenting with statue ideas. In this maquette of *Egypt Enlightening Asia*, the left arm is lifted and a scarf drapes the head and shoulders.

With a few changes the transformation into *Liberty Enlightening the World* began. The right arm is lifted and the left is lowered. The head scarf is gone and the robes have been changed.

He lifted one arm high, and then the other. He added details and then took them away. It took nearly four years, but at last he had a statue he could be proud of. Every feature was perfect, and rich with symbolic meaning.

Liberty Enlightening the World wore a long robe and sandals, patterned after the garments worn many centuries before by Libertas, the ancient Roman goddess of liberty. Her right hand held a torch, symbol of the light of liberty that she would bring to the world. Her left arm cradled a tablet, symbol of the rule of law in a democracy. At Laboulaye's suggestion, "JULY IV MDCCLXXVI" was inscribed on the tablet. It's the date (written in Roman numerals) of the signing of America's Declaration of Independence. At her feet lay a broken chain, symbolizing Lincoln's abolition of slavery.

Liberty's handsome face, modeled on Bartholdi's mother, looked out at the world with a calm, strong gaze. On her head she wore a crown in the shape of a seven-pointed sunburst, each ray representing a continent. From torch to toenails, Liberty was complete in every detail—but she was made of clay and stood just four feet tall.

In the finished design, the sunburst crown, the torch, and the tablet are in place.

It was fashionable for 19th century Parisians to have statues made of themselves, and Bartholdi was in great demand. He created hundreds of these small sculptures in his Paris studio while he waited for opportunities to do the colossal work he loved. He had studied painting before he turned to sculpture, and occasionally he picked up his brushes to create portraits such as the one on the easel of his mother, Charlotte Bartholdi.

Bartholdi had made the model on his own time and at his own expense, but he couldn't continue alone. To construct the colossal statue that he was planning, he would need skilled workers, tools, and expensive materials. Where would the money come from? He took the problem to Laboulaye.

Again the timing was right. Laboulaye had done everything he could to help establish the Third Republic. France's newest government was thriving, and he was free to turn his attention to the monument.

Laboulaye had many important friends in America as well as in France, and in 1875 he organized them into a group called the French American Union. The Union had one purpose: to build *Liberty Enlightening the World*. French members were responsible for raising funds for the statue itself; the members in America were to raise money for the pedestal that it would stand on. Laboulaye, as president of the Union, was responsible for everything.

Fund raising in France began enthusiastically. Union members gave benefit concerts and dinners, advertised for donations in newspapers throughout the country, and held a lottery. They found that it was not as easy to raise money for a gigantic statue as for a small medallion. The contributions were disappointing.

The fund raising campaign in America was even more disappointing—it didn't begin at all. The Americans waited—perhaps they weren't convinced that the monument would really be built. Laboulaye could see he faced an enormous challenge in the years ahead.

Meanwhile, in his studio, Bartholdi wrestled with a challenge of his own: how to turn the four-foot-tall model into a 151-foot-tall statue.

Wealthy donors who could afford to buy the expensive tickets attended the benefit concerts and dinners. People with less money donated to the statue by responding to the French American Union's newspaper ads.

Bartholdi knew that Liberty would outgrow his studio, so he moved the project across Paris to a spacious metal workshop on the rue de Chazelles. There, at the Gaget, Gauthier Company, the enlargement was carried out.

First, the clay model Ⓐ was carefully measured from all sides. To do this, a simple wooden frame Ⓑ was built around it. Then plumb lines, Ⓒ strings with weights attached to the ends, were hung evenly from the frame. The weights made the plumb lines hang perfectly straight, which made precise measurements possible. The workers measured from points on the statue, for example the tip of the nose, to the plumb lines, and they did this for hundreds of points. Then they re-did each measurement, just to be sure there were no mistakes. When they were satisfied, each measurement was multiplied by two.

Then a larger wooden frame Ⓓ was built and again plumb lines Ⓔ were hung. The second model Ⓕ was built inside that frame, using the doubled measurements and the plumb lines to make sure it was an accurate replica. The second model was too big to be made of heavy clay. Instead a wooden armature (framework) was built and covered with plaster.

Bartholdi studied the new model carefully. Features that had looked perfect on the small clay model didn't always look right on the larger plaster one, and he made many changes. When he was satisfied, workers repeated the process.

For the final stage of the enlargement, Bartholdi had to proceed differently. Even the Gaget, Gauthier factory couldn't contain a full-size, 151-foot-tall model. The statue was divided into sections and workers built plaster models of pieces of the statue. The right hand and torch Ⓖ was the first piece to be finished.

Work is in progress on the Liberty's left arm. The wooden armature of the sleeve has already been coated with plaster. The plaster dust has turned the worker sitting on it into a ghost! The hand and tablet will be coated next.

The hand and tablet have been plastered,
Bartholdi has made his final changes, and
Liberty's left arm is ready for the next step
in the process.

The factory was a busy, noisy place. Heaps of wood littered the floor and plaster dust filled the air. All around were pieces of Liberty—a torch here, a foot there, a section of robe propped against a wall. It was a strange sight indeed as Bartholdi and the workers moved through the clutter, dwarfed by the gigantic body parts.

Bartholdi had chosen to make the statue out of copper, and with good reason. It's a strong metal that can be rolled into thin sheets and easily bent and shaped. And copper has another unique quality that Bartholdi liked.

When a metal like iron is exposed to air and moisture, a chemical reaction called oxidation happens. Oxidation creates the reddish brown coating, called rust, which eventually weakens and destroys the iron. Copper oxidizes also, but instead of rust, a pale green coating called *verdigris* is produced. The color is beautiful, and verdigris actually protects the metal.

Flat sheets of copper were used for the statue, 340 of them in all. Each was about as thick as two pennies. They were shaped using an ancient metal-sculpting technique called *repoussé*. In repoussé, metal is hammered against a mold until it takes on the shape of the mold.

There were several steps in the repoussé process. First, using full-size plaster sections of the statue Ⓐ as guides, wooden molds Ⓑ were built to the exact shape of the plaster model. Then a sheet of copper Ⓒ was placed on the side of a mold that had taken on the shape of the plaster Ⓓ, and the repoussé process began. Hammering was done on only one side of the copper sheet so that the hammer marks Ⓔ would be hidden inside the statue. The side that was shown to the world Ⓕ would be smooth and unmarked. Finally, each finished piece of copper was braced on the inside with iron straps Ⓖ to make sure that the thin metal didn't bend or lose its shape.

Bartholdi took his problem to a brilliant young engineer named Gustave Eiffel. Eiffel had already made a name for himself building iron railroad bridges. His bridges looked delicate but they were strong enough to carry heavy freight trains.

The 151-foot-tall statue was a challenge even for Eiffel. The 42-foot-long right arm and torch, which stretched up, out, and away from the body, was especially hard to support. It took a year, but Eiffel devised a framework, a "skeleton" for Liberty that would keep her standing through the most violent New York storms.

The skeleton was a 96-foot-tall tower called a pylon. The massive 15-inch beams that ran from top to bottom at the four corners were the "spine." The "bones," hundreds of iron beams, were attached to the spine. And finally, Liberty's copper "skin" was attached to the bones.

Supporting the statue wasn't Eiffel's only problem. When two different metals, such as copper and iron, touch in the presence of certain liquids, such as salt water, a chemical reaction takes place that produces electricity. It's the same reaction that occurs in flashlight batteries. In the damp, salty air of New York Harbor, Liberty's iron skeleton and copper skin could have become the world's tallest battery, producing electricity that would have corroded the metal.

Eiffel figured out a way to keep the two metals apart by installing pads of asbestos between the copper and the iron.

(A) The four iron beams at the corners of the pylon tapered inward as they rose upward to their full height of 96 feet.

(B) Horizontal and diagonal iron beams were attached to the pylon to strengthen it.

(C) Smaller beams were the link between the pylon and the copper.

(D) Sheets of hammered copper were attached to the smaller beams.

(E) Wooden scaffolding was erected for workers to stand on.

Eiffel invented remarkable construction techniques for the statue that are still being used, but today he is best known for the famous structure in Paris that bears his name, the Eiffel Tower.

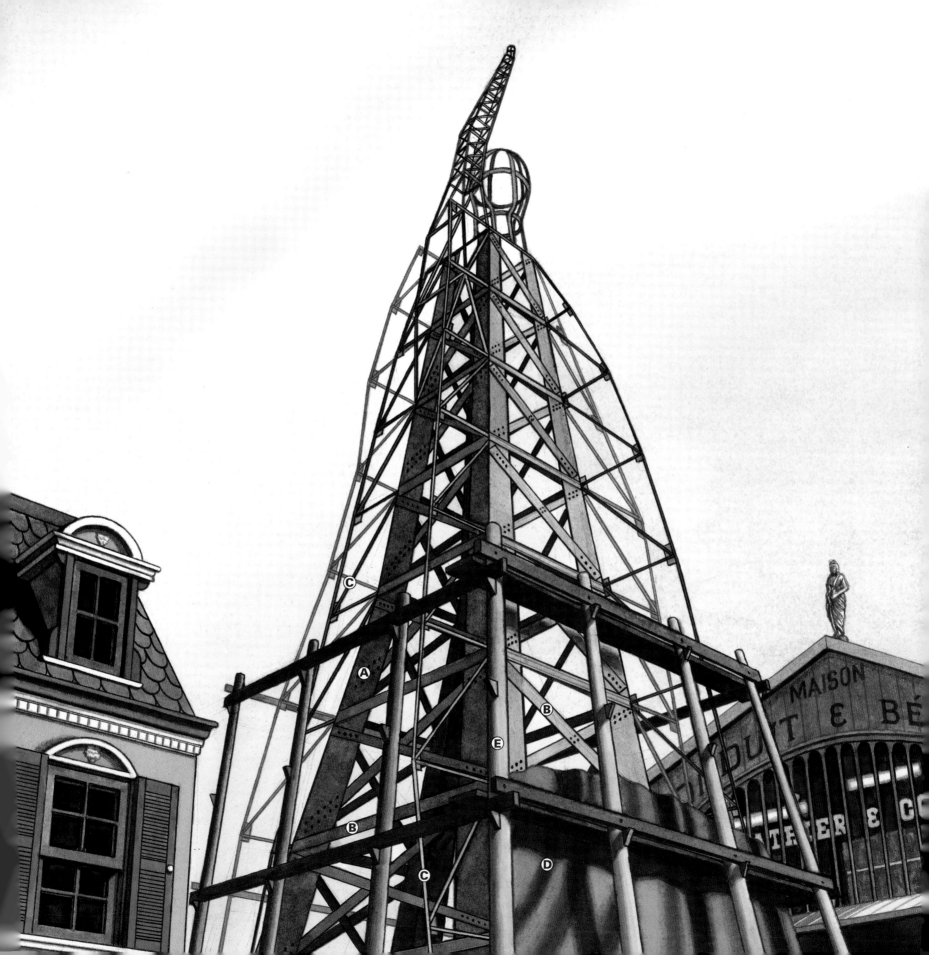

In 1880 Laboulaye and the French fundraisers met their goal! It had taken five years and tremendous effort, but they had collected $250,000, enough to finish the statue.

In 1881 Bartholdi was ready to have a look at his "American daughter." Workers began assembling Eiffel's iron framework outside the Gaget, Gauthier factory. In a ceremony on October 24, 1881, the first piece of copper was attached.

As the statue slowly rose skyward, curiosity mounted. Parisians wanted a closer look, and Bartholdi was happy to oblige. In July of 1882, he invited a few important guests to enter Liberty through the sole of her right foot, climb a staircase in her shin, and join him for an elegant meal served at a table inside her knee.

Less important folks were not offered lunch. They had to be content with a visit to the clanging, banging Gaget, Gauthier factory. Nearly 300,000 people visited while the statue was being constructed.

On May 25, 1883, after a long and full life, Edouard Laboulaye died. He didn't get to see the completed statue, but his other important dream had come true. The Third Republic, which he had worked so hard to create, was a successful, stable democracy. It governed until 1940, when Germany invaded France in World War II. Laboulaye's role in the Statue of Liberty is often overlooked but, without his original idea in 1865 and his fund raising work in the years after, it never would have been built.

A year later, on May 21, 1884, the statue was finished. Even without a pedestal, Liberty towered over the city. People and horses moved like ants past the hem of her copper robes. It was such an inspiring sight that the French government, which until then had not contributed a single franc to the statue, offered to pay the entire cost of shipping it to New York.

Unfortunately, there was no rush. Liberty was all dressed up, but she had nowhere to go. She stood patiently on the rue de Chazelles, and waited.

On the other side of the Atlantic, the Pedestal Committee fund raisers were struggling. They organized benefits of every kind: concerts, boxing matches, horse races, and dinners. They placed donation boxes on shop counters around the city. Bartholdi wrote a book to sell, and an American poet named Emma Lazarus wrote a poem. No matter what they tried, contributions only trickled in.

And on Bedloe's Island work on the pedestal was going slowly as well. Architect Richard Morris Hunt was hired to design it, and it took him over a year to come up with a plan that the Committee approved of.

Engineer Charles P. Stone was hired to build the pedestal, and he ran into problems right away. The stone walls of the eleven-sided fort were to remain, but the its foundation had to be dug out to make room for the pedestal's foundation. The excavation was not easy—the fort had been built to withstand whizzing cannonballs.

By the time Liberty was finished in Paris, only the pedestal's concrete foundation was in place in New York. With its twenty-foot-thick walls, the foundation was a great achievement—the largest mass of concrete of its time—but there was still much more to be done.

Then, during the winter of 1884, the pedestal work site was shut down. There was not enough money to pay the workers! Would Liberty ever stand on Bedloe's Island? No one knew.

Above: One of the many ways the Pedestal Committee raised money was by selling little replicas of the statue through newspaper ads.

Right: Cartoonists gleefully joined in the pedestal controversy.

Other cities took advantage of the uncertainty. Philadelphia, Boston, Cleveland, and San Francisco all stepped forward to offer the statue a home. Each claimed they could raise overnight the pedestal funds that New York hadn't been able to raise in a decade. Would Liberty end up in another city? No one knew.

Everyone, it seemed, had an opinion, and newspapers around the country printed many of them. Some people blamed the Pedestal Committee for their fund raising failure. Some people blamed New York businessmen for being too tight-fisted to donate. Some people said the statue should just stay in France.

In January of 1885, despite the ongoing debate, Bartholdi took a chance. He gave instructions to prepare Liberty for travel. It took half a year for workers to carefully take apart the statue, label all the pieces, pack them into 214 wooden crates, and load the crates onto the French navy ship *Isère*. While they worked, Bartholdi waited. Would his Liberty have a home? He didn't know.

THE STATUE OF LIBERTY
AS IT WILL APPEAR BY THE TIME THE PEDESTAL IS FINISHED.

On March 12, 1885 Pedestal Committee members received some upsetting news. They had raised $182,000, but only $3,000 was left. Pedestal costs had risen, and they needed to raise another $100,000. It seemed like an impossible task. Work on Bedloe's Island might have to stop again, maybe forever.

The bad news traveled quickly. Newspaper publisher Joseph Pulitzer heard it the next day, Friday the 13th, and jumped into action. He was determined to save the Statue of Liberty. On March 16 he launched his own fund raising campaign in the pages of his newspaper, *The World*.

Pulitzer made the campaign entertaining for his readers. In editorials and cartoons, he mocked the millionaires who hadn't donated and praised the ordinary, hard-working Americans who had. He honored every contributor, adults and children alike, by printing their names, and sometimes their letters, in *The World* for all to see.

JOSEPH PULITZER

When Joseph Pulitzer arrived from Hungary in 1864, he had no money, knew no one and spoke no English. Twenty years later he was a wealthy newspaper publisher. He believed his success was made possible by the freedom he found in his adopted country. He was happy to help build a statue honoring American liberty.

The World. MARCH 22, 1885

THE PEDESTAL FUND JUMPS NEARLY $1200 IN A SINGLE DAY

"The World" Gives $1000 and Sets an Example—Hearty Response All Along the Line—
Sure Signs of an Earnest Resolve to Prepare a Place for Liberty's Feet.

To the Editor of The World:
We children, brother and sister, send the sum of 10 cents for the benefit of the pedestal fund for the Statue of Liberty.
—Nellie H. and Frank O. Farnam

To the Editor of The World:
I am a little girl nine years old and would like to do something for the Statue Fund. I will send you a pair of my pet game bantams if you will sell them and give the money to the Statue.
—Florence De Forest

To the Editor of The World:
I enclose $1' as my subscription to the Bartholdi Statue Fund. I wanted to send more but my papa said $1 was enough from a little boy five years old.
—Yours respectfully, Willie H.

To the Editor of The World:
Kindly regarding our old-time ally and yet unchanged friend, France, and in the sacred names of Liberty and its glorious exponent, guardian and defender, Democracy. I subscribe the enclosed $5 towards elevating the Standard of Right.
—Mount Vernon, NY.

Pulitzer's enthusiasm was infectious, and it changed the way people felt about the statue. He persuaded Americans that it was a gift of lasting importance and an honor to the whole country, not just New York.

Readers responded generously. In just one month, Pulitzer raised $25,000. By May 16, 1885 he had raised another $25,000. Other newspapers followed his example, and donations poured in from around the country.

By the time the *Isère* steamed through The Narrows on June 17, 1885 more than a hundred ships, horns and whistles blaring, were waiting to escort her into New York Harbor. Cheering crowds lined the shore to welcome the ship and its precious cargo.

The excitement of Liberty's arrival could not change the fact that there was still no pedestal for her to stand on. The packing crates were put into storage on Bedloe's Island. Once again, Liberty would have to wait.

UNCLE SAM'S AWKWARDNESS

NEW ARRIVAL FROM FRANCE— "Ah Monsieur Oncle Sam! Escort me to my pedestal, s'il vous plaît."

UNCLE SAM— "H'm. Well, you see, the fact is Miss Liberty, we've only had ten years notice to get the tarnation thing ready, so it isn't quite finished yet."

On the morning of October 28 a million people watched a parade in New York City in Bartholdi's honor. That afternoon the sculptor was whisked by boat to Bedloe's Island for the ceremony. An enormous French flag covered Liberty's face, and Bartholdi had been given the honor of performing the official unveiling. He entered the foundation and began climbing the winding staircase in the center of the statue. After 354 steps he arrived inside the head.

Above him, a steady rain drummed against the copper. From below he could hear band music and 2,500 excited people, special guests who had been invited to Bedloe's Island for the event, noisily finding their seats. Thousands more people, just as excited and noisy, crowded the decks of the battleships and barges and yachts and fishing boats that circled the island.

Looking up the East River past the jostling boats, Bartholdi could make out the three-year-old Brooklyn Bridge through the fog and rain. His Liberty, 28 feet taller, now replaced it as the tallest structure in New York Harbor. We can only imagine his thoughts as he waited that day.

The speeches went on and on. At last Bartholdi released the flag and cheers exploded from the crowd. Steam whistles and bells and foghorns from over 300 boats split the air. The sound was deafening.

Bartholdi's American daughter was home at last.

Left: As big as she was, Liberty was hard to see during the October 28 celebration. Steam from boat engines and smoke from cannon salutes combined with the rain to create a dense fog.

Right: In the confusion of the festivities, Bartholdi unveiled Liberty early, in the middle of a senator's speech. The cheering crowd drowned out the senator and the rest of the ceremony.

As the years passed, Liberty's dark copper skin slowly oxidized to a pale green verdigris. Americans forgot Bartholdi's name, forgot that the statue honored the friendship between the French and the Americans. The United States was changing, and the meaning of the statue was changing as well.

In 1892 the first Federal Immigration Station opened on Ellis Island, half a mile from Bedloe's Island. Ellis Island was the first stop in America for millions of Europeans seeking new lives. These were the people Emma Lazarus wrote about in 1883. For these immigrants, as they sailed past, necks craning, the statue represented the freedom they had crossed an ocean to find.

Today Bedloe's Island is called Liberty Island. Ellis Island is no longer an immigration station, and passenger ships from Europe no longer steam past the statue. Now ferry boats from New York and New Jersey carry millions of people every year to Liberty Island to visit the world's tallest statue.

Bartholdi's creation has become America's most famous landmark, instantly recognized everywhere as the symbol of democracy and freedom. Liberty truly does enlighten the world.

THE NEW COLOSSUS

NOT LIKE THE BRAZEN GIANT OF GREEK FAME
WITH CONQUERING LIMBS ASTRIDE FROM LAND TO LAND;
HERE AT OUR SEA-WASHED SUNSET-GATES SHALL STAND
A MIGHTY WOMAN WITH A TORCH, WHOSE FLAME
IS THE IMPRISONED LIGHTNING, AND HER NAME
MOTHER OF EXILES, FROM HER BEACON-HAND
GLOWS WORLD-WIDE WELCOME, HER MILD EYES COMMAND
THE AIR-BRIDGED HARBOR THAT TWIN-CITIES FRAME.
"KEEP, ANCIENT LANDS, YOUR STORIED POMP," CRIES SHE
WITH SILENT LIPS, GIVE ME YOUR TIRED, YOUR POOR,
YOUR HUDDLED MASSES YEARNING TO BREATHE FREE.
THE WRETCHED REFUSE OF YOUR TEEMING SHORE;
SEND THESE, THE HOMELESS, TEMPEST-TOST TO ME,
I LIFT MY LAMP BESIDE THE GOLDEN DOOR!

EMMA LAZARUS

FRÉDÉRIC AUGUSTE BARTHOLDI

Bartholdi returned to France where he was greeted as a hero, just as he had been in the United States. He had given nearly two decades of his life to the statue, and he had spent $20,000 of his own money, a vast sum at that time, but he had no regrets. As he said, "The dream of my life is accomplished."

He lived quietly in Paris with his wife and his mother. In the evenings he would play the violin while his mother accompanied him on the piano. Though his greatest accomplishment was behind him, he continued to work as an artist. He finished his last sculpture just weeks before his death on October 4, 1904.

TIMELINE

7.4.1776	United States Declaration of Independence
1789	French Revolution
1811	Edouard Laboulaye born (died 1883)
1834	Frédéric Auguste Bartholdi born (died 1904)
1852	Louis Napoleon declares himself Emperor Napoleon III
1856	Bartholdi visits Egypt
1865	Laboulaye suggests a gift to America
1867-69	Bartholdi works on *Egypt Enlightening Asia*
1870	Napoleon III declares war on Prussia
1871	Prussia defeats France
1871	Bartholdi travels to America
1875	Third Republic established in France
1875	Laboulaye organizes the French American Union
1876	Liberty's arm and torch displayed at the Philadelphia Centennial Exposition
1878	Liberty's head displayed in Paris
1880	French fundraisers reach goal of $250,000
1881	Workers begin erecting Eiffel's framework in Paris
1882	Luncheon served inside Liberty's left knee
1883	Work begins on Bedloe's Island
1883-84	Statue on display in Paris
3.16.1885	Pulitzer starts fundraising campaign in *The World*
6.17.1885	*Isère* delivers Liberty to America
8.11.1885	Pulitzer campaign and Pedestal Committee reach fundraising goal of $282,000
4.22.1886	Charles P. Stone completes pedestal
10.28.1886	Statue of Liberty Opening Ceremony

GLOSSARY

Armature—framework

JULY IV MDCCLXXVI—July 4, 1776

Maquette—preliminary model for a sculpture

Oxidation—chemical reaction that can occur when a metal is exposed to the air

Pylon—tapering metal support tower

Repoussé—sculpting technique in which thin sheets of metal are hammered against a mold to shape them

Republic—democracy in which elected officials govern the people who elect them

Verdigris—green coating that forms on copper when it oxidizes

Liberty Island is now a National Park run by the National Parks Service. Their website is an excellent source of information. http://www.nps.gov/stli/index.htm

STATUE FACTS

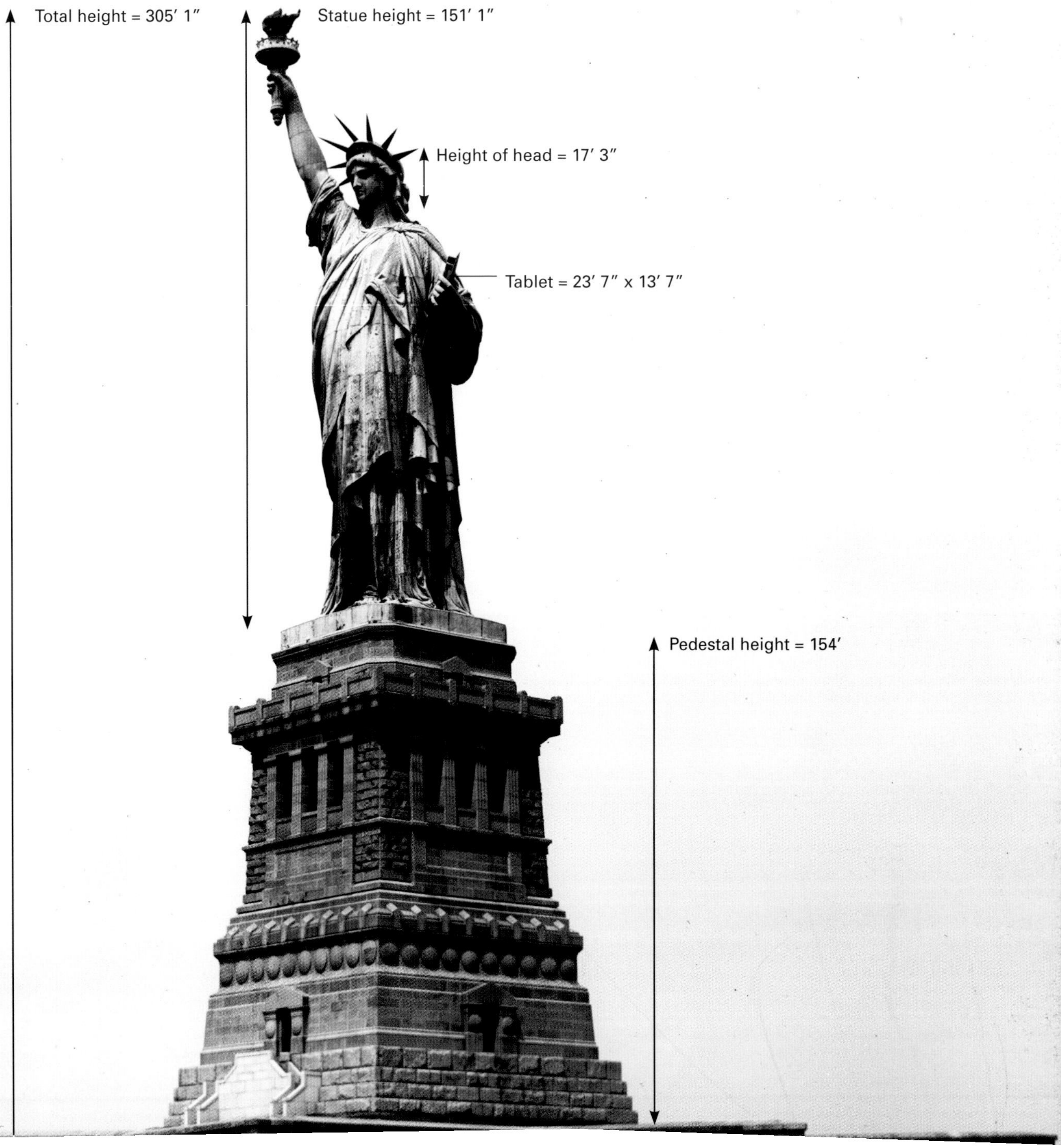
Total height = 305′ 1″
Statue height = 151′ 1″
Height of head = 17′ 3″
Tablet = 23′ 7″ x 13′ 7″
Pedestal height = 154′

Width of eye = 2′ 6″

Length of nose = 4′ 6″

Length of index finger = 8′

Fingernail = 14″ x 10″

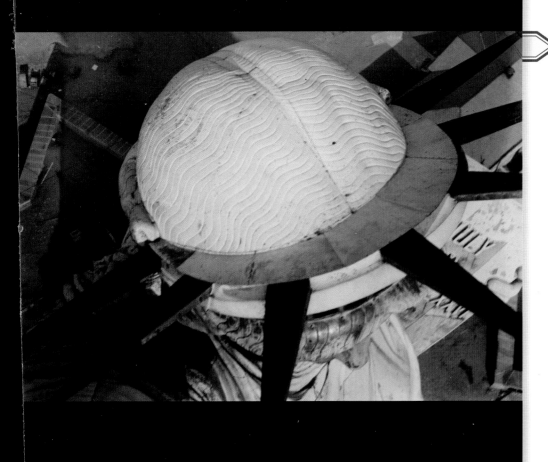

INDEX

SELECTED BIBLIOGRAPHY

Bartholdi, Frédéric Auguste. *The Statue of Liberty Enlightening the World*. New York: North American Review, 1885. Reissued New York: New York Bound, 1984.

Blanchet, Christian and Dard, Bertrand. *The Statue of Liberty: The First One Hundred Years*. New York: American Heritage, 1985.

Gilder, Rodman, *Statue of Liberty Enlightening the World*. New York: The New York Trust Company, 1943.

Gschaedler, Andre, *True Light on the Statue of Liberty and Its Creator*. Narberth, PA: Livingston Publishing Company, 1966.

Handlin, Oscar, *Statue of Liberty*. New York, NY: Newsweek Book Division, 1971.

Khan, Yasmin Sabina, *Enlightening the World: The Creation of the Statue of Liberty*. Ithaca, NY: Cornell University Press, 2010.

Moreno, Barry, *The Statue of Liberty (Images of America)*. Charleston, SC: Arcadia Publishing Company, 2004.

Moreno, Barry, *The Statue of Liberty Encyclopedia*. New York: Simon & Schuster, 2000.

Provoyeur, Pierre and Hargrove, June, *Liberty: The French-American Statue in Art and History*. New York: Harper and Row, Publishers, Inc., 1986.

Stone, Ross Conway, *A Way to See and Study the Statue of Liberty Enlightening the World*. Bullion Publishing, 1887

Trachtenberg, Marvin, *The Statue of Liberty*. New York: The Viking Press, 1976.

———◆———

PHOTO CREDITS

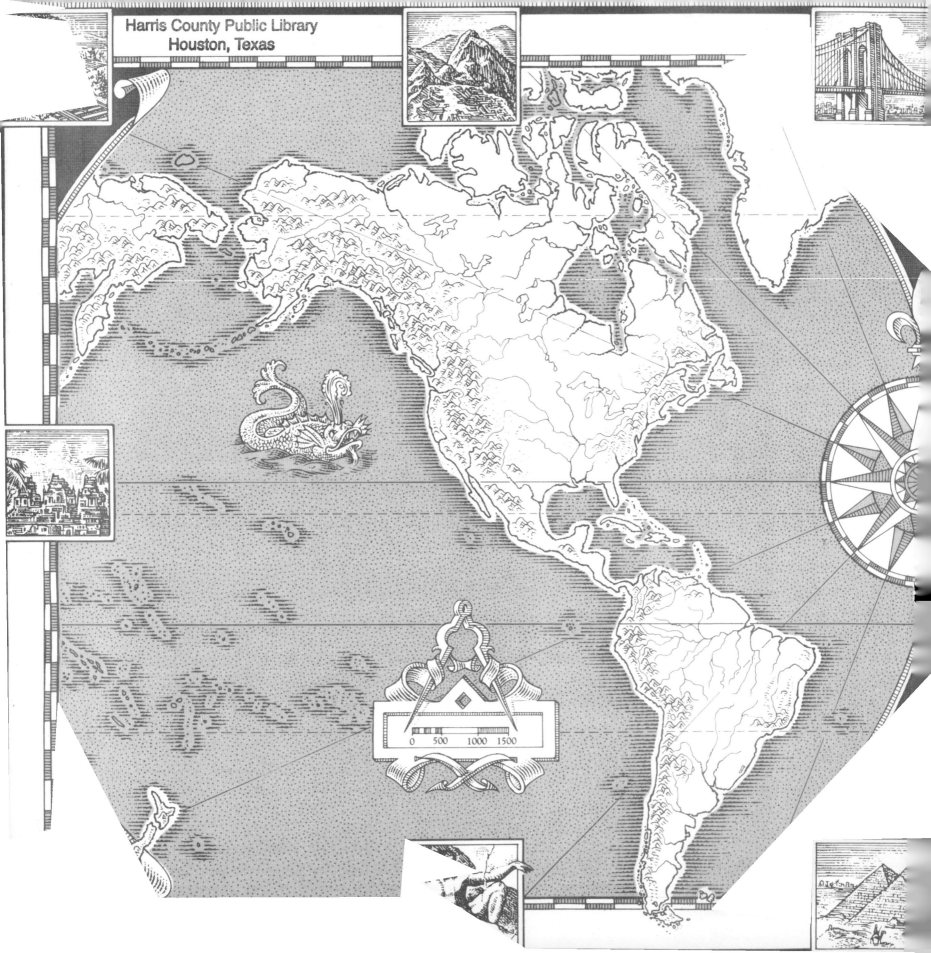

0 500 1000 1500